THE AMERICAS

KEITH LYE

GLOUCESTER PRESS
London · New York · Toronto · Sydney

CONTENTS

NORTH AMERICA	**4**
NORTH AMERICAN PEOPLES	6
NORTHERN NORTH AMERICA	8
CENTRAL AMERICA / CARIBBEAN	16
SOUTH AMERICA	**22**
SOUTH AMERICAN PEOPLES	24
NORTHERN SOUTH AMERICA	26
SOUTHERN SOUTH AMERICA	30
ANTARCTICA	**33**
ORGANIZATIONS	**34**
GLOSSARY	**35**
INDEX	**36**

How the maps work

This book has two main kinds of maps. Physical maps, such as that on pages 4 and 5, show what the land is like – indicating rivers (blue lines), mountain ranges (purple and dark brown), forests (dark green) and deserts (beige).

The red lines on the physical maps divide the regions which are dealt with in the individual chapters. Therefore, the shape of a region on the physical map corresponds to the shape of the region's political map.

The political maps, such as that on page 8, show the boundaries and names of all the countries in a region. Black squares indicate the location of the capital cities. Arranged around the maps are the flags of each country, together with the type of government, name of the capital city, population and land area.

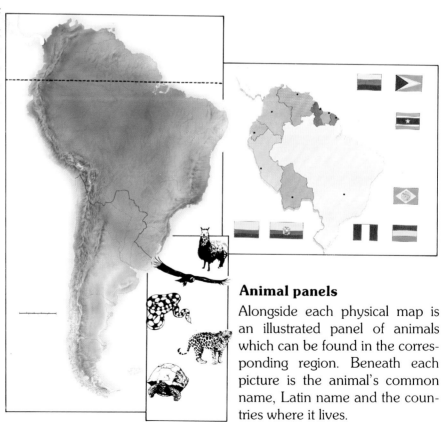

Animal panels

Alongside each physical map is an illustrated panel of animals which can be found in the corresponding region. Beneath each picture is the animal's common name, Latin name and the countries where it lives.

INTRODUCTION

North and South America are contrasting continents. They include the world's richest and most developed nation, the United States, and many developing countries, in some of which there is great poverty.

To compare the wealth and development of countries, a useful measure is the per capita gross national product, or the per capita GNP. This is the total value of all the goods and services produced by a country in a year, divided by the population. In 1984, the United States had a per capita GNP of US $15,490. By contrast, the per capita GNPs of Argentina and Brazil were US $2,230 and $1,700, respectively, but these two middle income developing countries are wealthy compared to Bolivia, whose 1984 GNP was $410.

The Americas are also regions of climatic contrasts, with the ice sheet of Greenland in the north and the steamy Amazonian forests on the equator. This book also discusses a third continent to the south of South America. This is Antarctica, the icy and windswept wasteland around the South Pole.

The Statue of Liberty in New York Harbour

Area: 24,258,375 sq km (9,366,212 sq miles).
Highest peak: Mount McKinley, in Alaska, 6,194 m (20,320 ft).
Lowest point on land: Death Valley, California: lowest point is 86 m (282 ft) below sea level.
Longest river: Mississippi-Missouri, 5,971 km (3,710 miles) long.
Largest lake: Lake Superior on the United States-Canadian border, 82,362 sq km (31,800 sq miles).

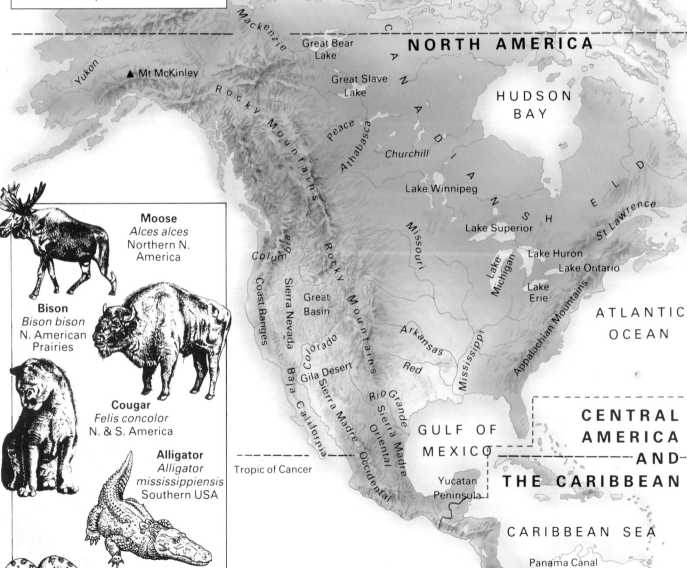

ARCTIC OCEAN

SCALE

| 0 | 400 | 800 Miles |

| 0 | 400 | 800 | 1200 Kilometres |

BEAUFORT SEA

Queen Elizabeth Islands

Ellesmere Island

BAFFIN BAY

Baffin Island

Victoria Island

Mackenzie

Great Bear Lake

NORTH AMERICA

Yukon

▲ Mt McKinley

Great Slave Lake

HUDSON BAY

Rocky Mountains

Peace

Athabasca

Churchill

C A N A D I A N   S H I E L D

Lake Winnipeg

St Lawrence

Columbia

Coast Ranges

Sierra Nevada

Great Basin

Rocky Mountains

Missouri

Lake Superior

Lake Michigan

Lake Huron

Lake Ontario

Lake Erie

ATLANTIC OCEAN

Colorado

Gila Desert

Arkansas

Red

Mississippi

Appalachian Mountains

Baja California

Sierra Madre Occidental

Rio Grande

Sierra Madre Oriental

GULF OF MEXICO

CENTRAL AMERICA AND THE CARIBBEAN

Tropic of Cancer

Yucatan Peninsula

CARIBBEAN SEA

PACIFIC OCEAN

Panama Canal

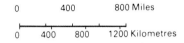

Moose
Alces alces
Northern N. America

Bison
Bison bison
N. American Prairies

Cougar
Felis concolor
N. & S. America

Alligator
Alligator mississippiensis
Southern USA

Eastern diamondback rattlesnake
Crotalus adamanteus
Eastern USA

North America is the third largest continent, after Asia and Africa. It includes Canada, the United States, Mexico, Central America and the Caribbean islands. It also includes the world's biggest island, Greenland, which lies in the cold and thinly populated Arctic region. Most of Greenland is buried under a huge ice sheet, the world's second largest after the ice sheet in Antarctica. Northern Canada also contains some smaller ice caps. But most of North America has a temperate climate, although part of Mexico is in the tropics. Central America and all the territories in the Caribbean, except for the Bahamas, are also in the tropics. This region, although much smaller, is generally more densely populated than the countries to the north.

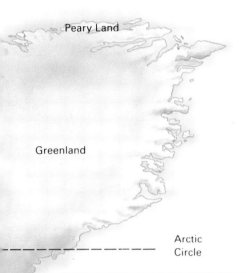

Peary Land

Greenland

Arctic Circle

Land and climate

Lofty mountain chains, including the Rockies, extend throughout all of western North America. Mountains extend into Mexico in the Sierra Madre ranges and active volcanoes rise in southern Mexico, Central America and the Caribbean. Plains separate the western mountains from the Appalachian range in the eastern United States. The Canadian Shield, around Hudson Bay, is an old mountain area which has been worn down to a flat lowland.

The far north is cold throughout the year, while the tropical south is always warm. But in between, much of North America has cold winters, warm or hot summers, and pleasant spring and autumn seasons. The rainfall varies. Mountain ranges near coasts and much of tropical North America are rainy. Deserts occur in rain shadow regions on the leeward sides of mountain ranges in the southwestern United States and in northern Mexico.

The snow-capped Rocky Mountains in Colorado

Tropical vegetation on a Caribbean island

NORTH AMERICAN PEOPLES

Population: 406,747,000.
Population density: 17 per sq km (43 per sq mile).
Largest cities:
Mexico City, Mex. 18,748,000
New York City, NY 7,165,000
Los Angeles, Cal. 3,097,000
Chicago, Ill. 2,992,000
Guadalajara, Mex. 2,587,000
Monterrey, Mex. 2,335,000

Until 500 years ago, North America was populated only by a few Eskimo hunters and by various American Indian groups. After 1492, when Christopher Columbus reached the "New World" of the Americas, the continent was colonized by Europeans. Most of the settlers in northern America were English speakers (with some French in Canada). The southern part of North America was occupied mainly by the Spaniards. Most of this southern region, including Mexico, is now part of what is called "Latin America", in which Spanish is still the chief language.

Ethnic groups

The earliest people of North America were the American Indians. Their ancestors arrived from Asia perhaps as long as 40,000 years ago. They spread throughout the Americas and founded several civilizations. The ancestors of the Eskimos also came from Asia, perhaps 12,000 years ago.

The Indian peoples of North America were conquered by the British, French and Spanish soldiers and settlers. Wars and contact with European diseases, to which they had no resistance, reduced their numbers. Today, American Indians and Eskimos make up only 1.6 per cent of Canada's population. In the United States, the Indians numbered 1.42 million in 1980. This was a major recovery from 1900, when there were only 237,000. In Mexico and Central America, intermarriage between Europeans and Indians has produced people of mixed descent, called mestizos.

Blacks, whose ancestors were transported from Africa to North America as slaves, are another important group. There are also sizeable communities of Asians, including Chinese and Japanese.

A Shoshone Indian chief in Wyoming

Most Americans are of European descent

Religion

More than 11 million Canadians are Roman Catholics, and most of the others are Protestants. Protestants form a majority in the United States, although Roman Catholics number more than 50 million. Most people in Mexico, Central America and the Caribbean (apart from the English- and Dutch-speaking islands) are Roman Catholics.

A Mormon (US Christian sect) temple, Utah

Languages

The official languages in North America are: English and French in Canada; English in the United States (although Spanish is also spoken) and Spanish in Mexico and most of Central America. The languages of the Caribbean include Spanish, English, French, Dutch and a dialect known as patois.

Black, white and Hispanic Americans play baseball

Ways of life

Canada and the United States, which has long been known as the "land of opportunity", are rich, developed countries. Most of their citizens have a high standard of living. But poverty still exists among some groups, including American Indians, blacks, and Latinos or Hispanic Americans (immigrants from Cuba, Mexico, Puerto Rico and other Spanish-speaking areas).

Mexico, Central America and the Caribbean are much poorer. Many people are peasant farmers and in Mexico people live, on average, ten years less than those in the United States.

A Mexican boy helps to herd goats

Population: 348,328,000.
Area: 23,497,195 sq km (9,072,318 sq miles).
Population density: 16 per sq km (42 per sq mile), excluding the sparsely inhabited island of Greenland.
Economy: The per capita gross national product (1984) was US $12,400. The United States had a per capita GNP of $15,490 and Canada $13,140. By contrast, the developing country of Mexico had the low per capita GNP of $2,060.

The land north of Central America includes three huge nations: Canada, the world's second largest in area; the United States, the world's fourth largest in area and population; and Mexico. It also contains Greenland, a thinly populated, self-governing Danish county, and two dependencies: British Bermuda and French St Pierre and Miquelon.

North America has plenty of fertile farmland and huge mineral resources. It produces more than a quarter of the world's manufactured goods, yet vast areas remain unspoiled wilderness and almost empty of people.

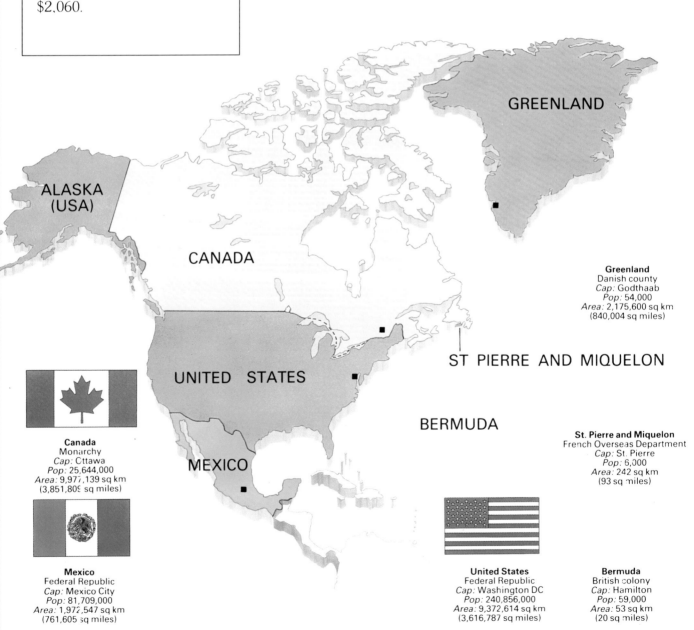

GREENLAND

ALASKA (USA)

CANADA

Greenland
Danish county
Cap: Godthaab
Pop: 54,000
Area: 2,175,600 sq km
(840,004 sq miles)

ST PIERRE AND MIQUELON

UNITED STATES

BERMUDA

St. Pierre and Miquelon
French Overseas Department
Cap: St. Pierre
Pop: 6,000
Area: 242 sq km
(93 sq miles)

MEXICO

Canada
Monarchy
Cap: Ottawa
Pop: 25,644,000
Area: 9,977,139 sq km
(3,851,809 sq miles)

Mexico
Federal Republic
Cap: Mexico City
Pop: 81,709,000
Area: 1,972,547 sq km
(761,605 sq miles)

United States
Federal Republic
Cap: Washington DC
Pop: 240,856,000
Area: 9,372,614 sq km
(3,616,787 sq miles)

Bermuda
British colony
Cap: Hamilton
Pop: 59,000
Area: 53 sq km
(20 sq miles)

Varied climate

The average January temperature in Yellowknife, on the Great Slave Lake, Canada, is −26°C (−15°F), as compared with 22°C (72°F) in southern Mexico. As a result, the land changes from ice sheets in the north to treeless tundra, through coniferous and deciduous forest to evergreen rain forest in the south. There are semiarid prairies and some desert. Many desert features, such as mesas and buttes, were originally worn out by rivers at a time when the climate was wetter than today. Wind-blown sand often erodes the land in deserts. It wears away softer rocks and carves strange rock forms.

Tall grasses up to 1.8 m (6 ft) high formed the original vegetation of the flat prairie land. Today much of it has been cultivated to grow vast acreages of wheat and maize. Summer temperatures on the prairies may rise higher than 38°C (100°F), but in winter they fall to a freezing −34°C (−30°F). Most of the deserts are located in the southwestern United States and in northern Mexico. They include the strikingly coloured Painted Desert in Arizona, which extends for 320 km (200 miles) along the course of the Little Colorado River, and the Mojave, which covers 64,700 sq km (25,000 sq miles) of wasteland in southern California.

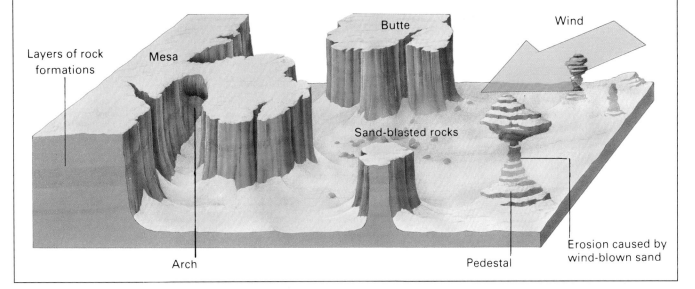

Layers of rock formations · Mesa · Butte · Wind · Arch · Sand-blasted rocks · Pedestal · Erosion caused by wind-blown sand

Contrasting landscape

The Great Lakes on the Canadian-US border were formed at the end of the last Ice Age, about 10,000 years ago. The lakes are drained by the St Lawrence River. Many other rivers rise in the Rocky Mountains, which make a barrier called the Great Divide. Most of northern North America's mountains formed when sideways movements in the Earth's crust squeezed rock layers into huge folds. Some mountains in Alaska, the far western United States and Mexico are volcanoes.

Mount McKinley in Alaska is North America's highest peak

The United States of America

The United States is made up of 50 states, plus the capital, Washington, D.C. (D.C. stands for District of Columbia, an area set aside by the federal, or central, government for the capital city.) Of the 50 states, 48 lie between Canada and Mexico. The others are Alaska, which was purchased from Russia in 1867 for US $7.2 million, and Hawaii. Hawaii consists of a group of islands in the North Pacific. It is over 3,200 km (2,000 miles) from California.

Most of the citizens of the United States are descended from people who emigrated there to seek a new life or who were taken there (mainly from Africa) as slaves. This has resulted in a mixture of ethnic types. In the 1980 census, 83.1 per cent of the people of the United States were of Caucasian (white) descent, 11.7 per cent were black, 1 per cent were Chinese, Japanese or Filipino, and 0.6 per cent were American Indian. Other groups included the Polynesians of Hawaii and Hispanic Americans.

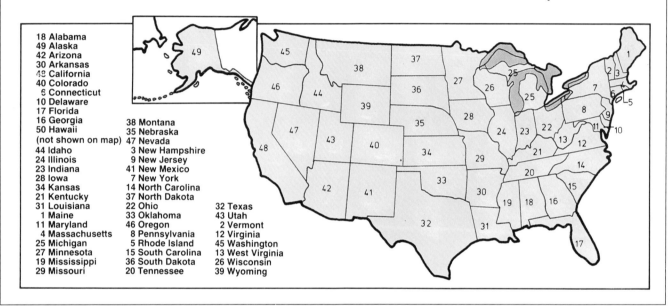

18 Alabama
49 Alaska
42 Arizona
30 Arkansas
48 California
40 Colorado
6 Connecticut
10 Delaware
17 Florida
16 Georgia
50 Hawaii
(not shown on map)
44 Idaho
24 Illinois
23 Indiana
28 Iowa
34 Kansas
21 Kentucky
31 Louisiana
1 Maine
11 Maryland
4 Massachusetts
25 Michigan
27 Minnesota
19 Mississippi
29 Missouri
38 Montana
35 Nebraska
47 Nevada
3 New Hampshire
9 New Jersey
41 New Mexico
7 New York
14 North Carolina
37 North Dakota
22 Ohio
33 Oklahoma
46 Oregon
8 Pennsylvania
5 Rhode Island
15 South Carolina
36 South Dakota
20 Tennessee
32 Texas
43 Utah
2 Vermont
12 Virginia
45 Washington
13 West Virginia
26 Wisconsin
39 Wyoming

Ways of life

Most of the people in the United States live in towns and cities, working in manufacturing or service industries. Farming – because of mechanization and efficiency – employs only 4 per cent of the workers, although it contributes 15 per cent to exports. The United States is the world's richest country, and only some of the oil-producing Middle Eastern nations have higher per capita GNPs. As a result, a majority of people enjoy a high standard of living, although there are minority groups of poorer people who have to use welfare services. Religious beliefs reflect the largely European origins of the people, most of whom (33%) are Protestants (mainly Baptists or Methodists) or Roman Catholics (23%). There are about 6 million Jews (2.5%), many of whom are from families who fled Europe in the 1930s.

US history is celebrated in Williamsburg, Virginia

Land of opportunity

Ever since European colonists began settling along the east coast during the 1600s, the United States has been rightly regarded as the land of opportunity. Soon more immigrants arrived from nearly every part of the world. The country declared its independence from Britain in 1776. Vast areas of land available for agriculture and grazing encouraged expansion westwards in the 1800s, sometimes accelerated (as in the 1840s) by the discovery of gold. Industrialization in the 19th century created urban employment and established the United States as a major world trading nation. Apart from the setback of the Depression in the 1930s, the country has continued to expand, particularly in the field of high-technology industries.

Wall Street Stock Exchange, New York City

Major Superpower

The United States is one of the world's two superpowers. It is the leader and the most powerful country in the Western alliance. This group of nations is opposed to the Communist world led by the other superpower, the Soviet Union. Since World War II ended in 1945, American troops have fought Communist forces in Korea (1950-53) and Vietnam (1964-73). Defeat in Vietnam made some Americans want to reduce their country's world role. But the United States continues to be involved in international affairs – including action against Communists in Central America, the Caribbean and South America – and plays a major role in the membership of the United Nations.

The United Nations headquarters, New York City

The Space Race

The United States and the Soviet Union were the first nations to commit major resources to space technology – which, during the 1960s, was often referred to as "the Space Race". The first artificial Earth satellite (1957) and the first man in space (April 1961) were Soviet achievements. The first American astronaut in space was Alan Shepard (May 1961), and eight years later it was the American Neil Armstrong who became the first man to walk on the Moon. In time, the two superpowers began to cooperate in space missions. The United States went on to introduce its Space Shuttle programme, which is designed to launch a variety of weather, survey and military satellites. The disastrous explosion of the Challenger Space Shuttle has suspended the programme until 1988. More recently, the Strategic Defence Initiative ("Star Wars") has begun development.

The Space Shuttle blasts off in a cloud of steam

Economy

Much of the power of the United States comes from its advanced technology. It has pioneered techniques such as assembly lines. mass production and automation. It is now a leader of computer technology. In the military field it exploded the first atomic bomb in 1945 and the first hydrogen bomb in 1952.

However. the major strength of the United States in an increasingly competitive world comes from its ability to be self-sufficient. American agriculture. industry and commerce together are able to produce enough food. goods and services for the whole country. Much of the industrial self-sufficiency in the United States is based on its vast fossil fuel and mineral resources.

The cost of any extra products that the nation chooses to import is more or less balanced by the value of the exports the United States sells to other countries. For example. the United States is the world's second leading oil producer. after the Soviet Union. although purchases of crude oil still account for about a fifth of all the country's imports. These have to be offset by the revenue gained from exports to countries such as Canada. Japan and Britain (which together take more than a third of US exported goods).

A machine harvests maize in the southern USA

United States Trade

Main sources of imports and exports:

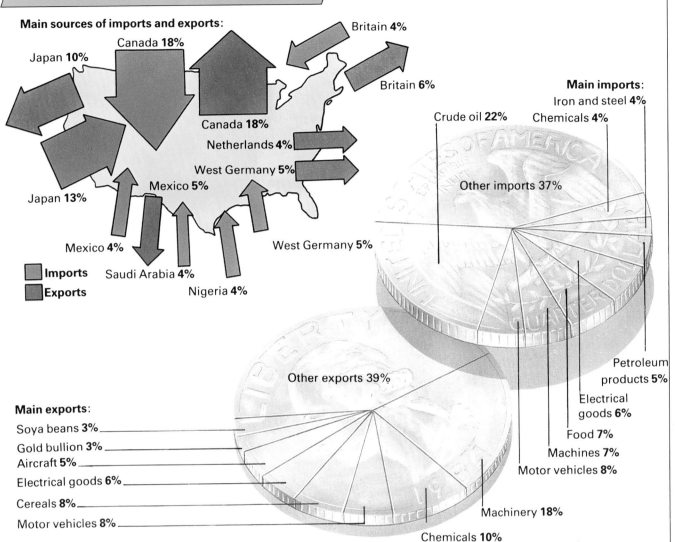

Japan **10%**
Canada **18%**
Britain **4%**
Britain **6%**
Canada **18%**
Netherlands **4%**
West Germany **5%**
Japan **13%**
Mexico **5%**
Mexico **4%**
West Germany **5%**
Saudi Arabia **4%**
Nigeria **4%**

- ▮ Imports
- ▮ Exports

Main imports:
Iron and steel **4%**
Chemicals **4%**
Crude oil **22%**
Other imports **37%**
Petroleum products **5%**
Electrical goods **6%**
Food **7%**
Machines **7%**
Motor vehicles **8%**
Machinery **18%**
Chemicals **10%**

Main exports:
Soya beans **3%**
Gold bullion **3%**
Aircraft **5%**
Electrical goods **6%**
Cereals **8%**
Motor vehicles **8%**
Other exports **39%**

The United States pioneered the assembly line

Silicon Valley, Calif., centre of the microchip industry

13

Canada

Canada, like the United States, is a self-governing, independent nation with a federal government. However, Queen Elizabeth II is recognized as the Queen of Canada and the country is therefore still formally a monarchy. The country is divided into ten provinces (each of which has its own government), and two thinly populated territories.

Like the United States, Canada is a land of immigrants and their descendants, most of whom came from Britain and France. For this reason, English and French are the chief languages in Canada today.

Canada has developed rapidly in recent years and from 1966 to 1986 its population increased by nearly 28 per cent.

The Canadian Parliament, Ottawa

Ways of life

Farming and forestry provide an outdoor way of life for about 5 per cent of Canadian workers. Most of the others work in factories, in service industries or in offices. It is a rich country and the majority of people are comparatively well paid. Less well off are some minority groups, such as the 368,000 Indians and about 50,000 Eskimos who are now more often known by the Eskimo word "Inuit". About two-thirds of the people speak English, 18 per cent speak only French, and 13 per cent speak both. Most French speakers live in the province of Quebec, which was originally explored and settled by French pioneers. In recent years, these language differences have led to conflict in Quebec.

English and French are spoken in Quebec, Canada

Eskimos (Inuits) hunting in northern Canada

Economy

Some outsiders mistakenly regard Canada as a northern satellite of the United States. But reference to the trading figures (page 13) shows that Canada exports to the United States as much as it imports. Canada is rich in natural resources and associated industrial output. Exports include minerals (from asbestos to zinc), wood pulp (nearly half of Canada has coniferous forests that yield timber for paper-making) and the products of the rich fisheries that surround the country. The Trans-Canada pipeline (which carries natural gas from the prairies to Montreal) is one of the longest in the world. Agriculture includes large-scale cattle ranching and the largest wheat- growing area.

Beef cattle in British Columbia, Canada

Mexico

In contrast to the United States and Canada, 37 per cent of Mexicans work on farms and are poorly paid. Some Mexicans illegally crossed the US border to look for better employment, although recently new US laws have forced many to return.

Mexico has many superb monuments, including huge pyramids built by the Aztecs, Mayans and other American Indian people. Hernán Cortés and his Spanish forces conquered Mexico in 1519-21 and destroyed the Aztec culture. The victorious Spaniards introduced Christianity and built many beautiful Roman Catholic churches. Today most Mexicans are Roman Catholics. Many are proud of their Indian heritage, and Christian festivals often show its influence.

A Roman Catholic church in Guadalupe, Mexico

Population: 58,419,000.
Area: 761,180 sq km (293,894 sq miles).
Population density: 77 per sq km (199 per sq mile).
Economy: The 1984 per capita GNP of the independent nations in this region was US $1,440, ranging from US $320 in Haiti to $7,140 in Trinidad and Tobago.

Central America and the Caribbean form the least developed parts of the Americas. Poor countries include Haiti, which had a per capita GNP of only US $320 in 1984, El Salvador ($710) and Guatemala ($1,120). Political instability, as well as natural disasters such as earthquakes, volcanic eruptions and hurricanes, are common. In Central America, only Costa Rica has had a stable democratic government for a long time. The United States plays a major part in the region's politics, especially by opposing left-wing Communist groups.

Guatemala
Republic
Cap: Guatemala City
Pop: 8,600,000
Area: 108,889 sq km
(42,042 sq miles)

Cuba
Republic
Cap: Havana
Pop: 10,221,000
Area: 114,524 sq km
(44, 218 sq miles)

The Bahamas
Monarchy
Cap: Nassau
Pop: 235,000
Area: 13,935 sq km
(5,380 sq miles)

Dominican Republic
Republic
Cap: Santo Domingo
Pop: 6,785,000
Area: 48,734 sq km
(18,816 sq miles)

St Christopher & Nevis
Monarchy
Cap: Basseterre
Pop: 40,000
Area: 262 sq km
(101 sq miles)

Belize
Monarchy
Cap: Belmopan
Pop: 168,000
Area: 22,965 sq km
(8,867 sq miles)

Haiti
Republic
Cap: Port-au-Prince
Pop: 5,870,000
Area: 27,750 sq km
(10,714 sq miles)

St. Lucia
Monarchy
Cap: Castries
Pop: 123,000
Area: 616 sq km
(238 sq miles)

Honduras
Republic
Cap: Tegucigalpa
Pop: 4,648,000
Area: 112,088 sq km
(43,277 sq miles)

El Salvador
Republic
Cap: San Salvador
Pop: 5,105,000
Area: 21,041 sq km
(8,124 sq miles)

THE
BAHAMAS
CUBA
DOMINICAN REPUBLIC
PUERTO RICO (USA)
HAITI
ANTIGUA
JAMAICA
AND BARBUD
ST CHRISTOPHER AND NEVIS
DOMINICA
ST LUCIA
GUATEMALA
BELIZE
HONDURAS
NICARAGUA
ST VINCENT
GRENADA
BARBADO
COSTA RICA
EL SALVADOR
PANAMA
TRINIDAD AND TOBAGO

Nicaragua
Republic
Cap: Managua
Pop: 3,342,000
Area: 130,000 sq km
(50,193 sq miles)

Costa Rica
Republic
Cap: San José
Pop: 2,714,000
Area: 50,700 sq km
(19,575 sq miles)

Panama
Republic
Cap: Panama City
Pop: 2,227,000
Area: 77,082 sq km
(29,762 sq miles)

Trinidad and Tobago
Republic
Cap: Port-of-Spain
Pop: 1,204,000
Area: 5,130 sq km
(1,981 sq miles)

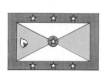

Grenada
Monarchy
Cap: Saint George's
Pop: 86,000
Area: 344 sq km
(133 sq miles)

Land and climate

Apart from the Bahamas, this region lies in the tropics. It is warm throughout the year. For example, the average temperature in Panama City in January is 26°C (79°F) and in July it is 27°C (81°F). The highlands are cooler. The rainfall is abundant and rain forest is common. Hurricanes, which form over the Atlantic Ocean, often batter the coasts.

Central America is a mostly mountainous land bridge, linking Mexico and Colombia. It contains active volcanoes, which are fuelled by underground pockets of magma (molten rock and hot gases). The Caribbean contains a chain of mainly volcanic islands. Some islands are made of coral. Their beautiful beaches and sunshine are major tourist attractions.

Puerto Rico
Commonwealth associated with the USA
Cap: San Juan
Pop: 3,197,000
Area: 8,897 sq km
(3,435 sq miles)

Jamaica
Monarchy
Cap: Kingston
Pop: 2,288,000
Area: 10,991 sq km
(4,244 sq miles)

St Vincent and the Grenadines
Monarchy
Cap: Kingstown
Pop: 103,000
Area: 388 sq km
(150 sq miles)

Antigua and Barbuda
Monarchy
Cap: St John's
Pop: 82,000
Area: 442 sq km
(171 sq miles)

Dominica
Republic
Cap: Roseau
Pop: 74,000
Area: 751 sq km
(290 sq miles)

Barbados
Monarchy
Cap: Bridgetown
Pop: 253,000
Area: 431 sq km
(166 sq miles)

Palm trees grow on a tropical beach in Haiti

Sugar cane being harvested in Barbados

Ways of life

The Indians of Central America founded several major civilizations long before Europeans arrived. Today, people of Indian origin form a majority in Guatemala, but mestizos dominate in El Salvador, Honduras, Nicaragua and Panama, with people of European descent forming a majority in Costa Rica. Many blacks live in Central America. They form the main group in Belize, which was known as British Honduras until it became independent in 1981.

Most of the Indians who lived in the Caribbean islands died during the early days of European colonization. Today, only a few Carib Indians survive in remote areas. Most people are of African or European descent, although there are some people of Chinese and East Indian origin. Caribbean culture reflects the age of colonization. For example, the English game of cricket is extremely popular on English-speaking islands.

Guatemalan farmers selling produce in a market

The West Indies play England at cricket in Jamaica

Earthquakes

Earthquakes occur when tectonic plates move. These plates are huge slabs of the lithosphere – the solid outer layer of the Earth. Some plates grind alongside each other, and the sudden jerky movement causes the ground to shake. The San Andreas fault in California is an example of this.

When two plates push against each other, one plate is pushed under the other. This occurs in the oceans, causing deep trenches, and giving rise to violent tremors.

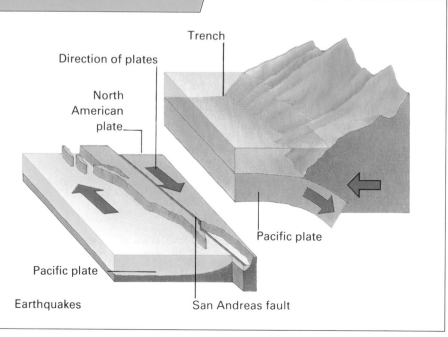

Trench

Direction of plates

North American plate

Pacific plate

Earthquakes

Pacific plate

San Andreas fault

Religion

Most people in Central America and the Caribbean are Roman Catholics, with Protestants being most numerous in English- and Dutch-speaking territories. Asian religions are also followed by various minority groups.

Voodoo is based on primitive African beliefs and is followed in Haiti. It is a form of witchcraft which involves the use of magic, charms and spells. Haiti's dictator from 1957 to 1971, Dr. François Duvalier (popularly known as Papa Doc), was an authority on voodoo. He used his knowledge to maintain his control over the people, who feared his magical powers.

Many West Indians are Rastafarians. Their religion is based on the worship of Ras Tafari, who became Emperor Haile Selassie I of Ethiopia.

People celebrating Easter in Sonsonate, El Salvador

U.S. influence

San Juan, Puerto Rico

The United States gives aid to many of its southern neighbours and supports anti-Communist groups. In the Caribbean, it gained Puerto Rico in the Spanish-American War of 1898 and it bought the Virgin Islands from Denmark in 1917. The people of these territories are US citizens.

The United States government is also concerned about political developments on other islands. It intervened to halt civil conflict in the Dominican Republic in both 1916-24 and 1965-6. In 1983, American troops invaded the small, formerly British island of Grenada to overthrow a Marxist government, following the murder of several government officials, including the prime minister.

Fidel Castro addresses a vast crowd

Cuba was Spanish territory until the Spanish-American War, when the United States helped Cuban rebels to end Spanish rule. American influence in Cuba remained strong until 1959, when guerrillas led by Fidel Castro overthrew a corrupt government. Castro made Cuba a socialist country, friendly to the USSR. In 1962, a plan to place Soviet missiles on Cuba nearly caused a world war.

Cuba helps left-wing movements in the Americas, including the Sandinista government of Nicaragua (named after patriot, General Sandino), which was set up in 1979. The United States opposes the Nicaraguan government and it has aided a guerrilla force, the Contras, in their attempts to overthrow it. The United States also helps the government of El Salvador, which is opposed by left-wing guerrillas. It also exerts influence in some countries, such as Honduras, through American companies, which play an important part in the economy. The United States paid for the building of the Panama Canal and ruled a strip of land called the Panama Canal Zone. This zone was given back to Panama in 1979. The United States will effectively control the Canal itself until 1999.

Nicaraguan soldiers prepare to patrol their border with Honduras

Economy

Farming employs just over half of the people of Central America. The most important crops are maize, coffee, cotton, bananas and citrus fruits. The forests yield valuable hardwoods. There is little mining and manufacturing is mostly on a small scale. Panama's economy depends heavily on the money it makes from ships using the Panama Canal. Opened in 1914, the canal is a short cut for vessels sailing between the Atlantic and Pacific oceans.

The Caribbean islands' leading occupations are farming and fishing. Bananas, sugar cane and tobacco are major crops, but many islands have to import food. Tourism is also important on islands such as Antigua, Barbados, Jamaica and the Bahamas, which lie close to the Florida coast of the United States. Cuba produces nickel and has large reserves of iron ore. Jamaica is the world's third leading producer of bauxite (aluminium ore), and gypsum (for making plaster) and silica (for glass) are also mined. Trinidad and Tobago, which has the region's highest per capita GNP (US $7,140 in 1984), produces natural asphalt, but crude oil accounts for 90 per cent of its exports. Manufacturing is increasing, especially in Cuba.

Workers tend young coffee plants in Guatemala

Mining bauxite, a chief export of Jamaica

A heavily laden container ship in the Panama Canal

SOUTH AMERICA

Area: 17,818,495 sq km (6,879,760 sq miles).
Highest peak: Aconcagua, 6,959 m (22,831 ft).
Longest river: Amazon, 6,437 km (4,000 miles); it also has the world's greatest volume.
Largest lake: Maracaibo, Venezuela, 13,512 sq km (5,217 sq miles).

South America is the world's fourth largest continent, after Asia, Africa and North America. The northern part is in the tropics, although the high mountains and plateaus of the Andes have bitterly cold climates. Southern South America ranges from warm, subtropical regions to the cold desert of Patagonia in the south.

South America consists of middle income, developing countries. The two largest, Argentina and Brazil, are developing quickly. They are expected to become major industrial powers in the 21st century.

Land and climate

The continent's most prominent feature is the huge Andes mountain range, which runs the entire length of western South America. It includes the highest peak in the Americas, Aconcagua. Many of the Andes' snow-capped peaks are active volcanoes.

The tropical north includes the world's largest rain forests, the *selvas* of the Amazon basin, where temperatures are always high and the annual rainfall averages 150-250 cm (59-98 inches). Drier tropical areas are covered by grasslands, called *llanos* or *campos*. One of the world's driest deserts, the Atacama, runs along the coasts of Peru and northern Chile, while the southeast contains temperate grasslands, including the *pampas* of Argentina. Patagonia is a cold desert plateau with little rain. The southern tip of South America, Cape Horn in Tierra del Fuego, is a land of storms.

The Amazon, the world's largest tropical rain forest

The *pampas* covers vast areas of Argentina

The dry, barren Atacama Desert in Chile

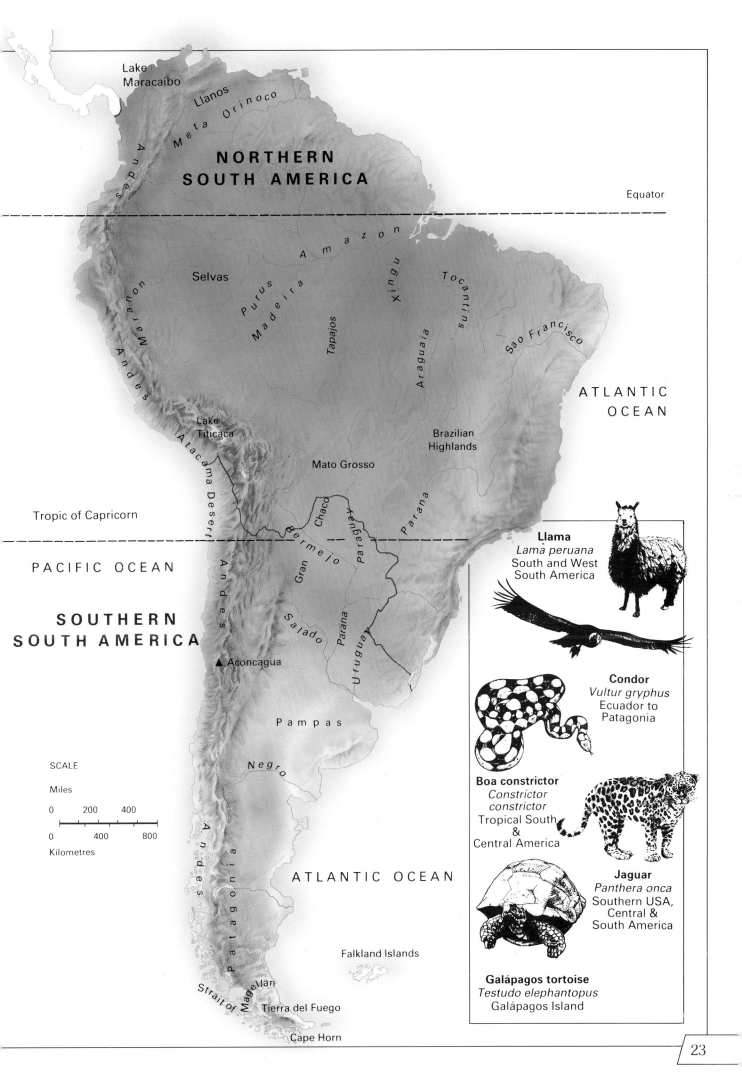

Lake
Maracaibo

Llanos

Meta
Orinoco

**NORTHERN
SOUTH AMERICA**

Equator

Andes

Magdalena

Amazon

Selvas

Purus

Madeira

Tapajos

Xingu

Araguaia

Tocantins

Sao Francisco

ATLANTIC
OCEAN

Andes

Lake
Titicaca

Atacama Desert

Brazilian
Highlands

Mato Grosso

Tropic of Capricorn

PACIFIC OCEAN

Chaco

Bermejo

Gran

Paraguay

Parana

**SOUTHERN
SOUTH AMERICA**

Andes

Salado

Parana

Uruguay

▲ Aconcagua

P a m p a s

Negro

SCALE

Miles

0	200	400

0	400	800

Kilometres

Andes

Patagonia

ATLANTIC OCEAN

Falkland Islands

Strait of Magellan

Tierra del Fuego

Cape Horn

Llama
Lama peruana
South and West
South America

Condor
Vultur gryphus
Ecuador to
Patagonia

Boa constrictor
*Constrictor
constrictor*
Tropical South
&
Central America

Jaguar
Panthera onca
Southern USA,
Central &
South America

Galápagos tortoise
Testudo elephantopus
Galápagos Island

23

SOUTH AMERICAN PEOPLES

Population: 278,991,000.
Population density: 16 per sq km (41 per sq mile).
Largest cities:

Buenos Aires, Argentina	9,677,000
São Paulo, Brazil	8,491,000
Rio de Janeiro, Brazil	5,094,000
Lima, Peru	4,528,000

The first inhabitants of South America were American Indians. They reached the continent perhaps 20,000 years ago and settled the southern tip of South America about 11,000 years ago. Some Indians were hunters, some were farmers, and some developed elaborate civilizations.

Spaniards conquered the great Inca civilization in the 1530s. Spain soon occupied most of the continent, with Portugal taking Brazil. In addition to Spanish and Portuguese, other official languages in South America include English in Guyana, Dutch in Surinam and French in French Guiana.

Ethnic groups

South American peoples include the American Indians, whites (who are mainly of Spanish and Portuguese origin) and blacks – the descendants of African slaves. There are also people of mixed origin, including many mestizos and mulattos. Mestizos are people of mixed European and American Indian origin. Mulattos are people of mixed African and European origin. Bolivia, Ecuador and Peru have large numbers of Indians. In Brazil, in 1900, there were about 230 Indian groups, each with its own language. About 90 groups have since become extinct. This is partly because of exposure to the diseases of foreigners who are now working in the forests.

Whites form a majority in the populations of Argentina, Brazil and Uruguay, while Chile, Colombia, Paraguay and Venezuela have large numbers of mestizos. Blacks and mulattos form large groups in the tropical countries, notably Brazil, Colombia, French Guiana, Guyana, Surinam and Venezuela.

A South American Indian family in Brazil

A Peruvian woman carries her baby on her back

Religion

The former Spanish territories of South America and the Portuguese territory of Brazil became independent in the early 19th century. But Roman Catholicism remains the chief religion. Protestantism is important in Guyana, which was formerly British Guiana until it became independent in 1966, and in Surinam, which became independent from the Netherlands in 1975.

In some countries, ancient Indian beliefs have influenced Christian worship and its festivals. In Brazil, many blacks follow a local religion, macumba, which combines African beliefs with Roman Catholicism.

The ornate altar of a Roman Catholic church in Quito, Ecuador

Ways of life

Farming employs 28 per cent of South America's workforce. But most farmers are poor. In recent years many people have moved into the towns and cities, hoping for jobs and better welfare services. Today, 68 per cent of South Americans live in urban areas. There is an enormous gap between the ways of life of the wealthy few and the unemployed masses in nearby slums.

The effect of poverty is felt in countries such as Bolivia, where people live, on average, only 53 years – that is, 23 years less than people in the United States. Yet most people enjoy the colourful fiestas held on national holidays. One of the best known is Rio de Janeiro's Carnival, which takes place before Lent. Parades and street dancing occur for four days and nights.

Many people in Peru have only poor housing

Carnival time in Rio de Janeiro, Brazil

Population: 228,476,000.
Area: 13,699,521 sq km (5,289,416 sq miles).
Population density: 17 per sq km (43 per sq mile).
Economy: The per capita GNP in 1984, excluding French Guiana, was US $1,670, and ranged from US $410 in Bolivia to US $3,520 in Surinam.

Northern South America contains eight independent republics and French Guiana. It includes the two poorest South American countries, Bolivia and Guyana, and the two richest, Surinam and Venezuela.

Brazil, the world's fifth largest country, makes up three-fifths of the area. It is a fast-changing nation. The exploitation of its great natural resources is involving the destruction of huge areas of forest, containing thousands of plants unknown to science, to make way for cattle ranches, mines and towns.

Venezuela
Republic
Cap: Caracas
Pop: 17,791,000
Area: 912,050 sq km
(352,145 sq miles)

Guyana
Cooperative Republic
Cap: Georgetown
Pop: 771,000
Area: 214,969 sq km
(83,000 sq miles)

Surinam
Republic
Cap: Paramaribo
Pop: 381,000
Area: 163,265 sq km
(63,037 sq miles)

French Guiana
French Overseas Department
Cap: Cayenne
Pop: 88,000
Area: 91,000 sq km
(35,135 sq miles)

Brazil
Federal Republic
Cap: Brasilia
Pop: 143,277,000
Area: 8,511,965 sq km
(3,286,488 sq miles)

Colombia
Republic
Cap: Bogotá
Pop: 29,956,000
Area: 1,138,914 sq km
(439,737 sq miles)

Ecuador
Republic
Cap: Quito
Pop: 9,647,000
Area: 283,561 sq km
(109,484 sq miles)

Peru
Republic
Cap: Lima
Pop: 20,207,000
Area: 1,285,216 sq km
(496,225 sq miles)

Bolivia
Republic
Cap: La Paz
Pop: 6,358,000
Area: 1,098,581 sq km
(424,165 sq miles)

Land and climate

The world's biggest river basin, that of the Amazon, covers 7,045,000 sq km (2,720,000 sq miles). Around the basin, with its hot, wet climate, are the cooler Guiana Highlands in the northwest, the Brazilian Highlands in the southeast and the Andes range in the west. The Andes Mountains are broadest in Peru and Bolivia, on whose border is Lake Titicaca. This is the world's highest lake with regular boat services.

The rain forests of the Amazon basin are the home of scattered Indian groups. Some live by farming, using the slash and burn system. They cut down or burn the trees on a small plot in the forest and grow crops. Eventually the crops exhaust the soil's goodness, and when yields fall the Indians move on to a new plot. However, the present destruction for commercial forestry is on such a large scale that valuable woodland is being lost forever.

The mighty Amazon River meanders to the sea

Indians fishing on Lake Titicaca, Bolivia

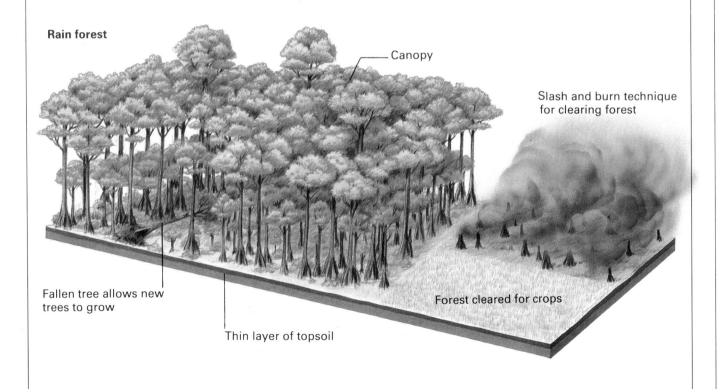

Rain forest

Canopy

Slash and burn technique for clearing forest

Fallen tree allows new trees to grow

Thin layer of topsoil

Forest cleared for crops

Ancient civilization: The Incas

The Inca civilization began in the 1430s in the Andes region. At its height, it stretched from what is now Colombia, through Ecuador, Peru and Bolivia, into Chile and Argentina. The Incas had an excellent road network, and used pack animals such as llamas for transport. The Incas also built great stone palaces and towns, such as Machu Picchu, with irrigation works and steplike farm terraces down hillsides. The Incas had a complex political system and made superb objects from gold and silver. These attracted the Spanish adventurers who conquered the empire in the 1530s. They seized its treasures and melted down the gold and silver objects. The Indians were enslaved and many died. But their heritage still lives on today.

The ancient city of Machu Picchu, Peru

Recent history

Since the early 19th century, when most South American countries became independent, the continent has had a disturbed history. Most nations have been extremely unstable politically. Long wars have occurred, elected governments have been overthrown by military groups, and brutal dictators have seized power and used torture to terrorize their opponents. One example of political instability is Bolivia. This country has had 190 governments in only 150 years.

Many political problems are caused by poverty. Left-wing guerrillas are operating in Colombia and Peru, where bombings, kidnappings and other acts of terrorism are common.

Bolivian troops discover an illicit cocaine factory

Economy

The region has many resources, including oil in Venezuela, Brazil, Ecuador, Peru and Colombia; bauxite in Brazil, Surinam and Guyana; iron ore, manganese and gold in Brazil; tin in Bolivia and silver in Peru. Many ores are exported and some are used in industries in cities such as São Paulo, Brazil. Farming is important. Brazil and Colombia are the world's top producers of coffee. Brazil is also a major producer of bananas, cattle, citrus fruits, cocoa, cotton, wood, corn, soya beans and sugar cane. The region faces many economical problems, including high inflation. In order to develop, the countries have borrowed large sums of money, and they must pay huge amounts of interest on these debts, which they find very difficult.

Ore processing plant in São Paulo, Brazil

Miners digging for tin in Bolivia

Venezuela has become a major oil producer

SOUTHERN SOUTH AMERICA

Population: 50,515,000.
Area: 4,118,974 sq km (1,590,344 sq miles).
Population density: 12 per sq km (32 per sq mile).
Economy: The per capita GNP in 1984, excluding the Falkland Islands, was US $2,020, ranging from US $1,250 in Paraguay to US $2,230 in Argentina.

Southern South America is made up of four independent countries and the British colony of the Falkland Islands. Argentina, the world's eighth largest country, occupies two-thirds of the region. Argentina and Brazil are South America's fastest developing countries, although rapid development has created many economic problems, including high inflation and massive debts.

Spanish is the official language of the four mainland countries and Roman Catholicism is the chief religion. More than 80 per cent of the people of Argentina, Chile and Uruguay live in cities and towns. But farming employs 49 per cent of the people of Paraguay.

Argentina
Republic
Cap: Buenos Aires
Pop: 31,186,000
Area: 2,766,889 sq km
(1,068,302 sq miles)

Uruguay
Republic
Cap: Montevideo
Pop: 2,947,000
Area: 176,215 sq km
(68,037 sq miles)

Falkland Islands
British colony
Cap: Stanley
Pop: 2,000
Area: 12,173 sq km
(4,700 sq miles)

Chile
Republic
Cap: Santiago
Pop: 12,261,000
Area: 756,945 sq km
(292,258 sq miles)

Paraguay
Republic
Cap: Asunción
Pop: 4,119,000
Area: 406,752 sq km
(157,048 sq miles)

Land and climate

The Andes Mountains form the backbone of southern South America. West of the mountains is the narrow country of Chile. The dry Atacama desert is in the north. The climate of central Chile, where most people live, is generally warm. The southernmost part is wet and stormy. Its jagged coast, lined by rocky islands, has been shaped by glaciers, and contains many deep fiords.

Northern Paraguay is in the tropics. It includes part of the Gran Chaco, which extends into northern Argentina. These plains are the hottest place in South America. Central Argentina and Uruguay contain huge temperate plains, with cattle ranches. Patagonia in southern Argentina is cold and dry. The southern tip of Chile and Argentina, including the stormy Cape Horn, is bitterly cold.

Patagonia, Argentina, has desert wastelands

Cape Horn, the stormy south tip of South America

Fiord created by glacier

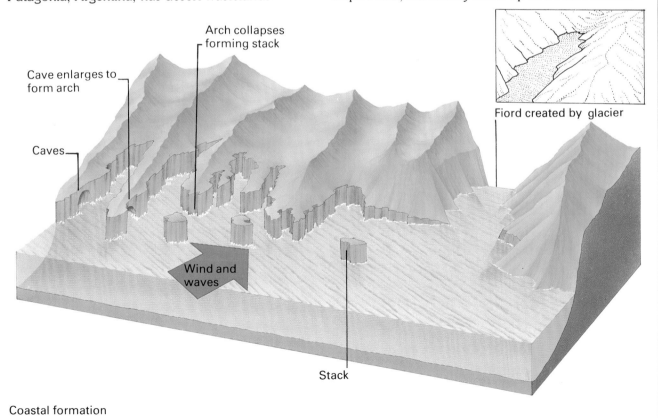

Arch collapses forming stack

Cave enlarges to form arch

Caves

Wind and waves

Stack

Coastal formation

Recent history

Argentina claims the Falkland Islands, which it calls the Islas Malvinas. Argentine troops invaded the islands in April 1982, but Britain recaptured them in the following June. Defeat in the Falklands and severe economic problems led to the collapse of Argentina's military government. Elections were held in 1983.

The other countries in the region also have problems. Chile elected a Marxist (Communist) government in 1970. Its opponents, aided by the United States, seized power in 1973. A harsh military regime has ruled ever since. Paraguay also has military rulers who permit little opposition. Although Uruguay has suffered under military dictators, civilian rule was restored in 1984.

Young Argentine soldiers in the Falklands, 1982

Economy

South America's resources include oil (Argentina) and copper (Chile). Mining is unimportant in Paraguay and Uruguay. Argentina, Paraguay and Uruguay have vast cattle and sheep farms. Crops include cotton, maize (corn), soya beans and wheat.

Manufacturing is increasing in cities such as Buenos Aires. High inflation and unemployment have caused many problems. All the countries have huge debts. Uruguay has to spend more than 8 per cent of its total GNP every year on interest payments.

Gauchos (cowboys) herd cattle in Uruguay

Modern skyscrapers in Buenos Aires, Argentina

ANTARCTICA

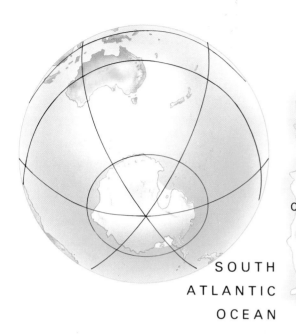

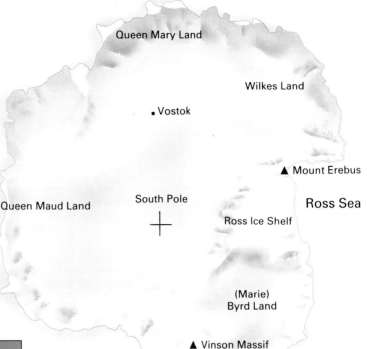

SOUTHERN OCEAN

Queen Mary Land

Wilkes Land

Vostok

Mount Erebus

Queen Maud Land

South Pole

Ross Ice Shelf

Ross Sea

SOUTH
ATLANTIC
OCEAN

(Marie)
Byrd Land

Vinson Massif

Weddell Sea

Antarctic Peninsula

SOUTH PACIFIC
OCEAN

South Shetland
Islands

Wintry sunshine at a scientific station

Antarctica is the fifth largest continent. It has an area of 13,209,000 sq km (5,100,000 sq miles), and is therefore larger than either Europe or Australasia. But most of the land is buried under the world's biggest ice sheet, although parts of the coast and some mountaintops, called nunataks, are ice-free. The highest peak is the Vinson Massif.

The ice in Antarctica totals about 25 million cubic km (6 million cubic miles). It is up to 4 km (2.5 miles) thick in places. Parts of the ice sheet extend beyond the land and form ice shelves over the sea. Parts of these shelves break away and form large, flat-topped icebergs.

Antarctica contains the South Pole and is the coldest continent. The world's lowest recorded temperature (measured out of the wind) was −89.2°C (−128.6°F). It was recorded at the Russian Vostok research station. The only people in Antarctica are scientists, who spend short spells working there. Various nations claim parts of Antarctica, but none of the claims has been agreed internationally.

ORGANIZATIONS

Several organizations work to further cooperation and economic development in the Americas. The Organization of American States (OAS), founded in 1948, has the largest membership. It seeks peace, security and cooperation among American nations. It includes the United States and also the representatives of some governments of which the United States disapproves. The Contadora Group, set up in 1983, has tried to negotiate between the US and Nicaraguan governments.

Organizations aimed at creating economic cooperation include the Central American Common Market (CACM), the Caribbean Community (CARICOM) and the Latin American Integration Association (LAIA).

Delegates at a meeting of CACM

CARICOM
Antigua and Barbuda
Bahamas
Barbados
Belize
Dominica
French Guiana
Grenada
Jamaica
Montserrat
St.Christopher and Nevis
St. Lucia
St. Vincent
Trinidad and Tobago

CACM
Costa Rica
El Salvador
Guatemala
Honduras
Nicaragua

CONTADORA
Colombia
Mexico
Panama
Venezuela

LAIA
Argentina
Bolivia
Brazil
Chile
Colombia
Ecuador
Mexico
Paraguay
Peru
Uruguay
Venezuela

OAS
Antigua and Barbuda
Argentina
Bahamas
Barbados
Bolivia
Brazil
Chile
Colombia
Costa Rica
Cuba
Dominica
Dominican Republic
El Salvador
Equador
Grenada
Guatemala
Haiti
Honduras
Jamaica
Mexico
Nicaragua
Panama
Paraguay
Peru
St. Christopher and Nevis
St. Lucia
St. Vincent and the Grenadines
Surinam
Trinidad and Tobago

USA
Uruguay
Venezuela

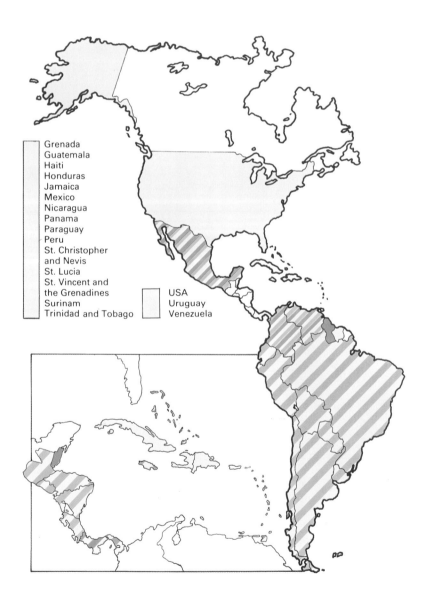

GLOSSARY

CLIMATE AND WEATHER
Hurricane Storm with very strong winds and heavy rain.
Polar climate Very cold, as in the Arctic and Antarctic.
Temperate climate Lacking extremes of temperature.
Tropical climate Found close to the Equator – hot all year round with abundant rainfall.

ECONOMIC SYSTEMS
Capitalist Individuals own the means of production, land, factories, etc. and employ other people to work for them to produce goods and services at a profit.
Communist The state (the 'people') owns and controls the means of production, in order to share more evenly the wealth created by their work.

ECONOMIC TERMS
Automation Automatically controlled process
Developed country One which is industrially and economically advanced.
Exports Goods sold outside the country in which they were produced.
Gross national product (GNP) The total value of all goods and services produced by a country (usually in a year).
Imports Goods from one country bought into another to be sold.
Industrialized nation One which has well developed industry as an important part of its economy.
Inflation Sudden rise in prices caused by the availability of too much money.
Manufactured goods Made from raw materials or individual components either by hand or by machines.
Mass production Manufacture of goods (often identical) in large quantities, often on a production line.
Resources Materials that meet a need, eg iron ore to make steel, or good soil for growing crops.

ETHNIC GROUPS
Blacks Negroid, belonging to a group of dark-skinned people.
Hispanic Relating to Spanish or Portuguese speaking people.
Inuit The Eskimo name for themselves, meaning the people.
Mestizo Person of mixed European and American Indian ancestry.
Mulatto Person of mixed Caucasian (white) and Negro (black) ancestry.
Whites Caucasian. Belonging to a group of white-skinned people.

GEOGRAPHICAL TERMS
Butte Small hill or mountain with very steep sides.
Campo Grassland plain in South America.
Coniferous forest Has cone-bearing trees (conifers).
Deciduous forest Has trees that lose their leaves in autumn.

Desert Region with little rainfall and few plants and animals, usually sandy. It may be either hot or cold.
Fiord Deep, narrow, steep-sided bay on the coast created by the action of glaciers.
Glacier
llanos Spanish term for open grassy plain.
Magma Molten rock material from within the earth.
Mesa Small steep-sided hill with level top.
Nunatak Mountaintop in Antarctica.
Pampa Extensive grass-covered plain of temperate South America.
Population density Average number of people living in a square kilometre (or mile), calculated by dividing the population of a country by its area.
Prairie Large area of rolling land that is fertile.
Rural Based in the countryside rather than in the towns.
Stack A column of rock detached from a cliff, seen on coastlines.
Tropical rainforest Forest in the tropics with trees that thrive on heavy rainfall, often called jungle.
Tundra Cold, treeless plain with little vegetation and wildlife found in Arctic regions.
Urban Based in towns rather than in the countryside.
Volcano Cone-shaped opening in the earth's crust through which molten rock (lava) comes to the surface.

RELIGIONS
Christianity Based on the teachings of Jesus Christ and his followers. Practised by Protestants, Roman Catholics etc.
Judaism Based on the teachings of Moses. Its followers are called Jews.
Mormon Member of the Church of Jesus Christ of Latter-Day Saints and Christian sect.
Rastafarian Followers of the Black Nationalist cult of Rasta Fari who later became Haile Selassie, Emperor of Ethiopia.
Voodoo System of beliefs originating in Africa involving magic, sorcery and mysterious rituals.

TYPES OF GOVERNMENT AND POLITICAL TERMS
Colony Place settled by people who go to live there but who remain citizens of their country of birth.
Coup Sudden seizure of power from an elected government by a group such as the military.
Federation Formation of a union often of states.
Guerrillas Soldiers who are not part of a regular army but who harrass the enemy by surprise raids and sabotage.
Military government Sometimes unelected, supported by the force of the military.
Monarchy Government by a monarch (king or queen). In some, the power is limited, as in Britain or Sweden.
Republic Country in which the people elect the head of state and the government.

All entries in bold are found in the Glossary

Aconcagua 22
Africa 5, 10
Alaska 9, 10
Amazon 3, 22, 27
Andes 22, 27, 31
Antarctica 33
    map 33
Appalachian range 5
Arctic 5
Argentina 3, 22, 28, 30
Arizona 9
Armstrong, Neil 12

Bahamas 5, 17
Belize 18
Bermuda 8
Bolivia 3, 25, 26, 27, 29
Brazil 3, 22, 24, 26, 29
British Columbia 15
Buenos Aires 32

California 10
Canada 5, 8, 10, 14
Cape Horn 22
Caribbean
    see Central America
Castro, Fidel 20
Central America and
    Carribean
    5, 16, 18
    economy 16, 20
    history 20
    map 16
    population 16
    religion 19
Challenger Space Shuttle 12
Chile 22, 28, 30
climate **35**
Colorado 5
Colombia 28, 29
Columbus, Christopher 6
contras 20
Costa Rica 18
Cuba 20

Death Valley 4
Denmark 19
Dominican Republic 19

earthquake 18

economic systems and terms
    35
Ecuador 28, 29
El Salvador 18, 19, 20
Elizabeth II, Queen 14
Emperor Haile Salassie 19
eskimo 6, 14
Ethiopia 19
ethnic groups **35**

Falkland Islands 30
French Guiana 24, 26

geographical terms **35**
government, types and
    terms **35**
Gran Chaco 31
Great Lakes 9
Great Slave Lakes 9
Greenland 3, 5, 8
Grenada 19
Guadalupe 15
guerrilla 20, 28
Guyana 24, 26, 29

Haiti 16
Hawaii 10
Honduras 18, 20
Hudson Bay 5
Incas 28
Indians 6, 14, 18, 24, 27
Inuit 14
Islas Malvinas 32

Jamaica 18

Korea 11

Lake Superior 4
Lake Titicaca 27
Latin America 6
Little Colorado River 9
Machu Picchu 28
Maracaibo 22
Mexico 5, 8, 10, 15
Miquelon 8
Mississippi-Missouri 4
Mojave 9
Mormon temple 7
Mount McKinley 4, 8

New York 3
New York City 11
Nicaragua 18, 20
North America 5
    climate 5
    ethnic groups 6
    language 7
    largest cities 6
    map 4
    population 6
    religion 7
North Pacific 10
Northern North America 8
    climate 9
    economy 8
    map 8
    population 8
Northern South America 26
    area 26
    climate 27
    economy 26, 29
    history 28
    map 26
    population 26

Panama 17, 18
Panama Canal 20
Paraguay 31
Patagonia 22
patois 7
Peru 22, 25, 27, 29
Protestants 7, 19, 25
Painted Desert 9

Quebec 14
Queen Elizabeth II 14
Quito 25

Rastafarians 19, **35**
religions **35**
resources **35**
Rio de Janeiro 25
Rocky Mountains 5, 9
Roman Catholic 7, 19, 25

Salassie, Emperor Haile 19
Sandinista 20
São Paulo 29
Shepherd, Alan 12
Shoshone Indian 6

Sierra Madre 5
Sonsonate 19
South America 22
    area 22
    climate 22
    ethnic groups 24
    largest cities 24
    map 23
    population 24
    religion 25
Southern South America 30
    climate 31
    economy 30, 32
    history 32
    map 30
    population 30
South Pole 33
Space Race 12
Spain 24
Spanish-American War 19,
    20
Statue of Liberty 3
Strategic Defence Initiative
    12
St Lawrence River 9
St Pierre 8
Surinam 24, 26

tectonic plates 18
Tierra del Fuego 22

United Nations 11
United States of America 5,
    8, 10, 20
    economy 12
    GNP 10
    map 10
    religion 10
    trade 12
Uruguay 30

Venezuela 22, 26, 29
Vietnam 11
Virgin Islands 19

Wall Street 11
Washington DC 10
Wyoming 6

Yellownife 9

Photographic Credits:
Cover, title page and pages 5 (both), 7 (right), 14 (right), 15 (bottom), 21 (top), 22 (top and right), 25 (top), 31 (right) and 32 (left and right): Zefa; pages 6 (left), 13 (both), 19 (bottom), 24 (right), 25 (left), 27 (right) and 28 (top): Tony Stone Associates; pages 6 (right), 7 (left) and 33: Spectrum; pages 7 (bottom), 9, 11 (top), 14 (top and left), 15 (top), 17 (both), 20 (top), 21 (right), 22 (left) and 29 (top and right): Robert Harding; pages 11 (bottom), 12 (right) and 18 (right): Art Directors; pages 18 (left), 19 (top), 20 (bottom), 21 (left), 24 (left), 25 (right), 29 (left) and 31 (left): Hutchison Library; pages 10, 28 (bottom), 32 (top) and 34: Frank Spooner Agency.